CHARICLES:

A DRAMATIC POEM.

BY THE

AUTHOR OF LYTERIA.

BOSTON:
TICKNOR AND FIELDS.
M DCCC LVI.

RIVERSIDE, CAMBRIDGE:
STEREOTYPED AND PRINTED BY
H. O. HOUGHTON AND COMPANY.

PREFACE.

The structure of the following drama is intended to resemble that of the Greek tragedy. It is written upon an event, rather than a plot; the scene is laid in the open air before the temporary abode of royalty, and the action is limited to a single night. The attempt has been made to invest a character with something of the dignity and moral power of the tragic chorus. The division into acts is in compliance with modern usage; the pauses being no longer than those that must be supposed in many of the best models of classic composition.

INTRODUCTION.

THERE are few instances of retributive justice more solemnly striking, than may be gathered from notices of the death of the third Cæsar, in the writings of Suetonius and Tacitus. A vigorous constitution, strengthened by the simple habits of early life, enabled Tiberius for a time to resist, not only the diseases that his later excesses poured upon him, but also the poison that was covertly administered by those in the interest of his successor. Stung and nettled by the taunts and execrations that arose about him, we read, that the dying tyrant would at one time strive to conceal the depth of his infamies, and at another, for very despair, would publish them in reckless bravado to the world. Feeble in body and a prey to superstitious fears, Tiberius journeyed for the last time towards Rome. Frightened by a fancied prodigy, and seized by mortal illness, that he dared not acknowlege to those about him, the emperor, when within sight of the city, turned suddenly, and gave the order to press back again to Capri. By increasing the extravagance of his debaucheries, by an occasional display of physical power, and by the constant scorn with which he affected to treat his physician, Charicles, the unhappy man sought to disguise his true condition from Caligula and his adherents. In vain, however, was every artifice—his death was too surely seen to be approaching; and finally Charicles acknowledged to those about him that the end must soon come. For this event measures were immediately taken—councils were held in private and despatches sent to the army and its commanders. Efforts were once made to induce Tiberius to appoint a successor; but even in the agonies of death, he grasped the signet ring strongly upon his hand, and refused to allow it to be taken. Yet not only was the tortured monarch made to realize the plots formed against him, and the contempt of those who should have been bound to his interest by personal favor and lavish liberality; but a punishment of strange severity was reserved for him. For upon recovering from a fainting fit, that had been mistaken for death, he found Caligula clothed with the insignia of royalty, and surrounded by a band of fawning courtiers. The whole party, paralyzed with terror at his unexpected resuscitation, for a time gazed stupidly upon the maddened tyrant. Finally, Tiberius was thrown upon a bed, where, at the order of Macro, he was deprived of life by suffocation.

Most of the incidents, as will be seen by a reference to the note at the close of the volume, are to be found in the historians already mentioned. A slight dramatic license has been taken in their arrangement and amplification.

The characters of Tiberius and his successor are intended to be consistent with their historical representation—the former having, as we are assured, something of the scholar and the poet mingled with the voluptuary, the tyrant, and the atheist; and the latter screening at times his detestable qualities under a crafty pretence of modesty and moderation.

In writing the part of Charicles, who is simply mentioned as a physician in the train of Tiberius, not employed to prescribe, but assisting with friendly advice, the imagination may be allowed some liberty. So likewise in Ennia, the wife of Macro, historically known as mistress and promised empress of Caligula.

DRAMATIS PERSONÆ.

TIBERIUS.
CAIUS CÆSAR CALIGULA.
CHARICLES.
LUCULLUS.
CRASSUS.
ENNIA.

The scene is an open space before the villa of Lucullus. At the base of the hill upon which the villa stands, are buildings for the accommodation of soldiers, retainers, and others. The action commences about sunset.

ACT I.

Lucullus, Crassus.

LUCULLUS.

COMMANDS he then the shelter of our villa
For a night only?

CRASSUS.

This, I cannot tell;
For a strange madness sways Tiberius now,
And none may guess his pleasure; when we stood
Scarcely two leagues from Rome, with travel spent,
And joyed to see her domes and palaces
Indent our northern sky—the Emperor,
Gazing upon the city, staggered back
As if Fate's finger touched him;—straight he cried,
"Turn all our horses, we'll again to Capri!"
And so, unkemped and wearied, back we toil,
Till some fresh freak shall seize him, or till Death,

The only Brutus left these craven times,
Shall dare to strike the monster.

LUCULLUS.

Soft, I pray,
We may not yet give word unto the hope
That eager dwells within us.

CRASSUS.

Nay, the end
Hurries upon him, although desperate will
Still wields the body. At Circejus here,
In the full circus, when all eyes grew bright
As the speech faded on his rigid lip,
And pain's dull gripe wrinkled his face in sufferance,
Two massive lances from the guards he snatched,
Rushed to the front, and shouting to the crowd
"*Cæsar is mighty yet!*"—
With certain aim transfixed the panting boar,
That made the soldiers pastime. Nerving thus
His arm to one great effort that drained off
The dying strength of nature, back he reeled,
And carried by his hirelings, left the games
A shattered mass of grossness.

LUCULLUS.

Charicles
Was with him when he fell?

CRASSUS.

Yes; to recall
A life that crimsons the hard cheek of earth,
And shames the patient heaven! Strange it is
That wise physician—whose well-governed mind
And vigorous frame conjure the chains that time
Binds on his latter years, and show them garlands—
Strange such as he should use his hard-earned skill,
To cheat infernal gods of their ripe victim!

LUCULLUS.

'Tis whispered here that comradeship of youth,
When this luxurious reveller bore arms
Nobly against the Germans, knit so close
The love of Charicles to this our tyrant,
That now,—of all the crowd of sycophants,
Soldiers, relations, courtesans, who press
About the dying monarch,—he alone
Stands firm and faithful to keep back the throng,

Who curse the lagging energies of life,
And aid the fates to do their welcome office.

CRASSUS.

The ring of soldier's steel breaks from below!
The horsemen, that by some half-hour precede
The Emperor, already fill the court.

LUCULLUS.

Can he be Macro who still sits his steed
While all descend about him?—no; he wants
The crafty courtesy that could supplant
The powerful Sejanus!—Dignity
That cannot palter, in his stillness lives.
A knight detains his stirrup—Ah, his step
To earth wears cautiousness like age. He speaks
To those about him, while he bares his head
In salutation. Whitened locks like those
Mark only one in all the monarch's train.
'Tis the physician Charicles!

CRASSUS.

His mien
Cannot be counterfeit: It is indeed

That brave old man who hither bends his steps.
The freshness and the vigorous trust of youth
Still cling about him, as the kindly vine
With its fond verdure wraps the storm-stripped trunk
In richer beauty, than when summer birds
Wantoned among its branches. He displays
A virtue not of impulse, or that temper
Whose native mien shows fairly,—but has grown
To all that men should honor by hard toil
And daily self-denial. As we praise
The fair conception that the artist strikes
From shapeless matter—rudely shivering
And tearing without pity through the rock,
Until his thought toils slowly into form—
So let us reverence him who doth not spare
To chafe and rend his being, till it shrink
To beauty more divine than any craft
Can mimic to the sense.

LUCULLUS.

This Charicles,—
So have I heard, and your report confirms,—
Deserves the high commending of a man
Who dares revere a truth, before the crowd

Are scourged to worship it,—whose loyalty
To true nobility ungarlanded
Is ever constant—yet whose generous heart
Hoodwinks his judgment to the benefit
Even of this Tiberius.

CRASSUS.

He is here;—
Few of our modern youth who climbed that hill
Would breathe so easily.

(*Enter Charicles.*)

You speed to-day;
We thought that Charicles could ill be spared
By his great patient. But perhaps even now
Rome's prayers are answered, and Tiberius lies
Beyond the help of leech-craft.

CHARICLES.

Sir, he lives;
And in a sudden gust of strength that Will
Drove through the shrinking fibres, spurned my aid,
And bade me quit his presence; lest the people,
While a physician waited at his side,
Should fancy Cæsar mortal!

CRASSUS.

Stay not then
A moment in this villa!—he will repent
This rashness, and again demand thy arm
To battle off his doom. Leave him to those
Who dare not stay the vengeance the high gods
Devise for their blasphemers.

CHARICLES.

I must not
Desert the final moments of a man
Whom friendship past has dowered with a claim,
That in his sad necessity dispels
The difference of years. We combatted
Together by the Rhine; and earlier still
In that fierce Rhætian war when the rough Alps
Leagued all their bulk against us. I have seen
Tiberius, tentless, stretched upon the earth,
While meanest soldiers with their blankets screened
Cold starlight from their faces! Through long nights
He gave command that any who had doubt
Of the next day's success, should break his rest,
And hear him tell again the well-laid plans

That promised victory. Our studies too
Waked better sympathy: the Cæsars hold
A spirit quick to seize what lesser men
By grappling and hard toil with grief attain,
And his bright wit, quick-flashing on the task,
Dispersed all doubts that shrouded the coy truth.

LUCULLUS.

Methinks that Charicles may claim discharge
From old indebtedness, in saving him
Whom Rome calls master, from a blacker deed
Than history shall whisper. I have heard,
From one who served at Capri, of a feast
Where poison lurking in the wine-brimmed cups,
Should banquet all to silence—had not he
Who planned this infamy, summoned in haste
A certain skilled physician, who prepared
An antidote, that saved the guilty man
From his own vile contriving.

CHARICLES.

Such report
May be as empty as the thousand tales
Men fable of their rulers. When we know

The open baseness of this sullied man,
We need not crimes that secret rumorers breathe
To make our pity fuller.

CRASSUS.

Hast thou then
No harsher word than pity, for this scourge
Of the vexed earth! this mercy-mocking fiend!

CHARICLES.

None, none, sir,—for he suffers. While the gods
Delayed their retribution, there was room
For other feeling. Now, when every grief
Pours on his naked head—when thick'ning pangs
Gnaw through the aching frame—and the hot thoughts,
Surging in chaos, rise and beat against
The rock where reason lingers—when the men,
Who fawned upon his greatness, plot his death—
And friendless, helpless Age in sorrow drifts
To that dark ocean, where unsightly wrecks
Of powers that cursed their holder, heave and toss
In ghastly impotence—then, anger melts,
Leaving compassion, awe, and tenderness.

CRASSUS.

Yonder are those untouched by any sense
That dulls their instant profit—Caius Cæsar,
And with him Ennia, whom he promises
Success shall make his empress!

CHARICLES.

Let me then
Withdraw unnoticed, for the Emperor
Must arrive speedily. I would put off
This garment soiled by travel, and prepare
To minister in these emergencies.

LUCULLUS.

Then follow, sir, our villa welcomes all—
Though Caius would not seek to shelter one
Who comes to guard what he, for greater cause
Than doth possess us all, plots to destroy;
While Macro's haughty and ungoverned wife,
Sold by her lord's ambition and her own,
Shall brook thy presence little:—So have care,
Her hate may prove most deadly!

CHARICLES.

Fear thee not;
For I have marked this woman, and observed
Her spirit swell beneath indignities,
Which to the world she carries mockingly.
In her there fails that mediating sense
To temper down the bright ideal of thought,
That it may warm to healthiness the life
Scorched by excess of lustre. She is formed
Of fine perceptions, through which every breath
Vibrates to joy or agony unknown
To coarse and passionless existences.
Such beings are developed in convulsion:
Their energies unused refuse to rust,
But do ferment and strive for mastership.
Strange, to confess the thousand accidents
That make us as we are!—Do we part here?

LUCULLUS.

This way for thee. I go below to greet
The Emperor: his coming will be sudden.
(*Exeunt Lucullus and Charicles.*)

CRASSUS.

How hardly stands the time when we must hail
These selfish plotters, who for private gain
Would push Tiberius to his eager grave,
As Rome's best patriots; when our fingers yearn
To doff our caps to this Caligula,
As one whose very blackness must show fair,
Contrasted with that arch-oppressor's wrongs,
That scourge the patient earth to bitterness!

(*Enter Caius Cæsar and Ennia.*)

CAIUS.

Ha, Crassus! Was it Charicles who left thee?

CRASSUS.

Ay, sir, he came but now.

CAIUS.

Mistake! mistake!
He should have fled to Rome—out of the reach
Of daily insult and indignity,
That pays his care to lengthen out a life,

Whose blood coins riches for the man who steals it.
Speed after him, say I have words to speak
That shall ring profit! Quickly bid him come!

[*Exit Crassus.*

Foiled by this man again! when I have gained
The popular voice, which may to-morrow call
A rival to take up the falling crown.
The guards, as yet fresh-bribed, are well prepared
To hail me monarch. 'Tis to-night—this night—
The sluggish deputation from the senate,
Bought by long fawning, should arrive to wait
His death, to call me instantly to fill
The lofty seat he drops from:—and this night
The old man dies! This must be compassed, *must*,
Despite this crafty leech who long enough
Hath shut us from our hope.

ENNIA.

Tiberius drained
The drugs that Macro mixed, and yet defies thee:—
Truly our Charicles bears spells that raise
Immortal aid to thwart thy purposes.

CAIUS.

He must be gained at any sacrifice;
And, Ennia, thou canst do it. Well I know
The crafty words and winning speciousness
Of a shrewd woman—and a fair one too.
Thy weapons are more delicate and sure,
Than bribes and threats that I might vainly use
In pressing this great suit.

ENNIA.

Here is one man
Might stand uncovered in the blaze of day,
And let the wholesome sunshine search him through,
To show no fleck upon him! Canst thou not
Find better uses for these purchased wiles,
Than to obscure the single honest light
By which we gauge our proper infamies!

CAIUS.

Waste not these doughty words on him who twirls
Thee and thy future as a brittle reed
Between his fingers! Thou art mine. Reflect
How I could bruise the life that I have sworn
Shall wear imperial greatness!

ENNIA.

As thou say'st,
I am most helpless. On and upward then—
It is my course and thine. If I have skill
In reading stubborn men, no promises
Of profit, or foreshadowed retribution
Can sway this Charicles—impregnable
On all parts, save that spot where honor waves
Her insubstantial sceptre. But let me
(If fortune so far help us) show him cause
Why this man's death must truly glorify
Him who invites it—show that both his gods
And feeble senators will count him blest,
Whose hand frees Rome from Capri's guilty lord,—
And he is ours to use!

CAIUS.

And having used,
To punish, for the days of hope deferred
That he hath cost us. I shall call thee empress
Ere the dead east shall redden; but to-night,
We work! No sleep or revel must intrude
Betwixt our deed and hope. We father still

The future in the present, and our fate
Is not stretched out before us, but is shot
By our own effort through the blank hereafter,
Where only fools run blindly. Charicles
Returns: to thy persuading I may owe
The crown we both shall wear. Be resolute
In every subtle art that captives men
From their own judgment. Ennia! I trust thee.

[*Exit Caius Cæsar.*

ENNIA.

I shall be faithful, and will have success
If mortal art can reach it. Then away,
Thou image and perception of a fate,
That wanders cruelly before my steps,
Showing a sad, calm glory which doth mock
My flushed and squandered being! Let me quell
The phantom, and press on—
And in a mazy whirl of vivid life,
Surfeit this restless soul. Our Charicles
Worships that servile spirit, which resigns
Fortune's best gifts for some fantastic good
Begot in reason's dotage. He bows not
With other men to the unbending will
Of him who triumphs; but refuses still

To pay the natural tribute which the crowd
Render stern purpose, that breaks destiny,
And dazzles men with what it steals from them.
He is of those to whom substantial things,
Clouded by fancy, seem as mockeries—
And who would sway the universe by dreams
That die upon their acting.

(*Enter Charicles.*)

It shows ill,
Physician, when such reverent locks appear
'Midst curled and scented parasites. We thought
That spurned by this mad patient, thou had'st fled
Beyond recalling, that his folly might
Glare on his dying eyes.

CHARICLES.

Until the last
I wait beside him. The physician sees
Poor nature stripped of all the snares she throws,
In her bright hours, for fickle sympathy.
All hearts can feel when loveliness is touched
With the quick shaft of sorrow—when the soul
Quits earth in perfumed robes of sentiment,
And genius, dolphin-like, from the dull lash

Of its own agony weaves robes of light,
And bleeds in changing beauty;—but when pain
Strikes vulgar want or selfish luxury,—
When the torn breast bares to the gazer's view
Vice, cruelty, and wretchedness, that strive
And mutiny 'gainst fainting reason,—then
'Tis our place to stand firmly, and support
With human pity what remains of man,
To kind oblivion.

ENNIA.

So dost thou wrong—
Snatching the healing cordials of the earth
To pour through bloated veins, while younger lives,
Still capable of good, perish unheeded!

CHARICLES.

He who hath knowledge to renerve the pulse,
May not thence arrogate the power to give
Or hold his skill, from any suffering.
All life alike claims his large sympathy:
The dews of heaven the sombre cypress feed,
Like the gay poppy.

ENNIA.

A starved Pestilence
Sits pressing his foul lip, and from his breath
Drinks hateful sustenance! Thy fatal spell,
That holds this sordid life, oppresses earth.
The senate has defied him, and the throng
Run wildly in the streets, and call aloud
That his dead bones—for oft his death is rumored—
Be thrown like carrion to the yellow stream
That cleanses Rome. *Tiberius to the Tiber*—
This is the cry that dies upon the breeze
That even now sweeps by us. As a god
Shall he be worshipped, who the state shall free
From this incumbent horror. Caius Cæsar,
Whom nobles, senate, people, long to crown,
Shall hold him in his heart, who boldly strikes
The blow to-night;—or but forgets to shield
Tiberius from the hands that are not shamed
To do their country service!—
Charicles,
I thought to have been temperate in my speech—
But craft and cautiousness fit not the time
Or business. Freely have I spoken;—so
Return thou answer.

CHARICLES.

The blanched locks I wear
Should cover no ambition. As the ear
Dulls to the harmonies of sense, the words
Of sober duty closely press themselves
About the listening heart. Transgression must
Scourge its fooled victim—though its knotted whips
Fret not those younger days, when our fresh strength
Leaps laughingly to pleasure's winning pipe.—
Thou art most beautiful;—I cannot think
That even Capri can have all debauched
A soul enshrined thus fairly. Do not seek
To bitter the high place that shall be thine
By shedding royal blood—tho' thick with guilt—
That thee and thine has patroned.

ENNIA.

While we speak,
The young Tiberius hurries to the side
Of the crazed dotard, who in some mad freak
May lift him to the throne;—then there must flow
More blood and richer, than supplies the veins
Of one shrunk tyrant!

CHARICLES.

Nay, if as thou say'st
The empire claim thy Caius for her lord,
Be sure that her great voice shall drown the cries
Of a dream-flattered youth. My daily craft
Has given skill to read the signs that Death
Stamps on the brow of the worn wretch he bids
To slumber in his chambers. Ere the sun
Shall thrice revisit us, this man shall lie
Beyond the thrust of malice. Do not snatch
So rudely at a life, that while we speak
Melts from between thy hope and its fulfilment.

(*Re-enter Caius Cæsar.*)

CAIUS.

Hast thou sped well? Speak, woman,
For our stained uncle, stung with pain and travel,
Now rages in the court! Physician, say,
Is our suit granted?

CHARICLES.

What is honest, sir,
There needs no suit to press. Proposals base

Cling not to my remembrance; and perchance
The sight of this grieved man, whose failing steps
His menials scarce support to where we stand,
Shall banish them from yours, and turn this guilt
To sober admiration at the doom
The god-defier tastes.

The Emperor!

(*Enter Tiberius, attended. He is followed by Lucullus, and many others.*)

TIBERIUS.

Hail, friends! Ha, Charicles, what brought thee here?
'Twas not my order. Take thy face from hence!
Our tree, though something bent, is still well sapped,
And needs no gardening. Speed thee to Rome—
There suck the purses of the credulous crowd,
The food of priests and doctors!

CHARICLES.

As a friend,
An early and a true one, I entreat
Your leave to tarry.

TIBERIUS.

As a friend, then, stay—
For we have need of such. 'Tis said the people
Armed with petitions, ay, and with clubs too,
Pour from the neighboring country to besiege
Our final night on their curst continent!
To-morrow's dawn embarks us all for Capri.
If thou dost stay, bewitch thy sober face
With wine and garlands; or if thou wilt deign
The reek of slaughter won with ruder arms
Than thy familiar physic—join my guards,
And hew these beggars to the thirsty earth,
Which from plebeian blood elaborates
A blooming vesture to out-do and shame
Our gewgawed lemans!

Orders were despatched
To have a banquet ready! Is it served?—
I have heard something of the sunny grape,
Whose essence cribbed in your sealed jars too long,
Craves resurrection to renew its summer
In these chilled hearts we bear. Am I not answered!
Is't ready! Ha!

LUCULLUS.

The nimble servants speed
With loyalty still anxious in your service.
Our tables bending with their choicest load
Shall soon invite your highness. But this coming
Was something sudden. We entreat your patience.

TIBERIUS.

'Twas not well done! Feasts constantly replenished
Should have awaited us. When we descend
From our fair island, and do deign to tread
The vulgar earth men live on, you should know
How Cæsar must be welcomed!
Ennia,
Mix for me wine as thou wert wont at Capri,
And bring it straight, for faintness is upon me! Haste, I say!
[*Exit Ennia.*
See there our doctor; how from far he smells
His chance of meddling profit. Keep thy drugs
For slaves and frightened women! Know our faintness
Is caused by travel—and already passes;
What canst thou do, poor leech!—fatten on fools!
When the time comes, we die.

CHARICLES.

Ay, sir, we die.
But if the time should lag, man can select
Some drug whose active potency is proved
Swift to wind up the hours;—and when the pulse
Strikes off a day at every maddening beat,
He can choose yet again, and with a drop,
Distilled from other vegetable life,
Undo the deadly errand of the first.
Holds Cæsar not, unrecognized, perchance,
Some old example in his memory
That fits the saying!

TIBERIUS.

Cease thy prating, peace!
I keep no memories:—but for a jest,
I'll practise thee with seeming, and feign aches
And knotted cramps, that shall thy craft o'erwhelm!
Say on this spot a gnawing horror pressed
Storming the seat of life, and sending forth,
'Gainst this dependency and that, fierce pains
That burned into the flesh. Say that this brow
Pent in a sullen madness, that must soon
Burst through the cracking flood-gates of the will,

And rage in every fibre—that this hand
Uncertain, palsied, could no longer clutch
The potency that warmed the sluggish clay
With a faint show of being—add to all
A tortured consciousness, weak to repel
The blazing thoughts that a blood-craving fate
Rained thick upon the brain !—If such a wretch,
Steeped thus in fullest aggregate of woe,
Cumbered the earth—what couldst thou do for him ?

CHARICLES.

Nothing ;—but smooth the painful path to death.

TIBERIUS.

Art thou foiled now ! drug then the foolish crowd—
When evils league to crush a monarch's life,
They scorn man's frail resistance. Yet thou know'st
We are yet free from pangs, that shall dispel
The soft enchantments of the sensuous world,
Ere we are called to leave it. Thou hast seen
This arm more truly hurl the death-fraught lance
Than any practised stripling. Well, sir, judge
Are we not Cæsar still !—only a little weary.

CHARICLES.

Seek stillness, then;—the only medicine
To soothe the ill thou bearest. Put away
This purposed madness of red revelry—
Relax the cords that bind thy troubled soul
To worldly pettiness. Withdraw apart—
For fickle sleep is soonest won alone.

TIBERIUS.

Alone! alone!—each nauseous drug thou own'st
Were sweet to such a horror. We have climbed
The Alpine heights together—grasping oft
The rugged shrub, whose roots more firmly cling
To their dead rock, than any gaudy flower
To the warm earth that feeds it:—thus it is
When every joy has perished, the starved heart
Cleaves with its total being to a world
Barren of any comfort. Solitude!
I loathe its deadly presence, and grow sick
Even as the brain now dreams it.
Charicles,
A word apart with thee, that the vexed soul
May cast the fiend that haunts it. Thou hast dreamed
Some show of truth in the weak jugglery

Fashioned by priestly knaves to drain their dupes!
Perchance to this foul tenement we hold
Thy folly gives a subtler principle
Than self-informing matter! Thy faint heart
Projects its best of being from itself,
And as a god adores it—as a god
Cursed and dethroned by all the miseries
That plough the world thou giv'st him. Nay, no word—
Till I have scared thee with a prodigy,
That shall out-wonder thy weak phantasy!
Thou hast beheld Apollo's marbled form
Stand in our hall at Capri—stand as fixed
As our strong watch-tower, whose deep-seated base
Grows to the stable earth. What thought hadst thou
When this perfection sunned thee with its life?

CHARICLES.

The thought of one whose study contemplates
Maimed and diseased mankind. In awe I stood
Before the stone-cast dream, that mirrored forth
A human form ransomed from every flaw
Prophetic of infirmity and death!
Long silently I marvelled;—till at length,
Drawing its fire from the fooled gazer's eye,

A consciousness divine inhabited
This shrine too noble for mortality.

TIBERIUS.

This image, sir—mark me, I pray thee now—
A mass of stone, dead, senseless, chilly, mute,
Ay, so thou think'st it,—heaved its rigid arm,
And, as alone in speechless trance I stood
Before the vital marble, breathed my name
In voice whose terrible music fills my soul;—
Which, for a moment's calmness, must yield up
The rash prediction to thy doubting ear.
"*God-mocking monarch*"—these the very words,
Echoed by night and day have they not sunk
Deep, deep into my being!—"*know the doom,*
That tardy justice for her scoffers rears,
Breaks on thy guilty head. No hand of thine
Shall place this spotless marble in the niche
Whereto 'tis destined! This stained island fly—
Thy friends desert thee—E'en the very stones,
That thou hast heaped in palaces and towers,
In fragments strew the earth! Away to die—
To die upon the shore whose tainted sands
Shall shame to hide thee!"

CHARICLES.

Sir, these sombre words
Were but the fancies of a troubled mind,
Which, sick with apprehension, turned its dreams
To horrors palpable.

TIBERIUS.

And thus thou think'st them—
Thou, so weakly duped!—
Teeming with boyish faith, thy heart can feel
The breath of deity in monstrous forms,
That strew the bitter earth. In stream and grove,
The slavish soul thou bearest paints a god,
Steeped in our human frailties;—hopes, fears, hates,
Loves, virtues, crimes, spawned of thy impotence,
Thou giv'st the natural essence named by thee
Creator, Jove, or Phœbus! Doubt this sense—
Question the miracle these eyes have seen!
Hug dead delusions—defraud reason still!

CHARICLES.

The studies I have followed, and yet more,
Such observation as our cautious craft

Hails as its best instructor, teach disease
May trick the eye with fancies, that shall grow
In the red light of frenzy—from the brain
Stealing a motion, form, and utterance,
To cheat the mind that 'gets them. Then distrust
The false impressions that the senses draw
From worlds of their creation. But go forth
When the pure soul, unscorched by feverish draughts,
Hovers from earth with every fervent note,
That swells in nature's anthem—there receive
Undoubting, such belief as the young breeze
Wafts in upon thy spirit. Know the calm
That falls so softly on the passive mind
Is not begot of falsehood!—know the Power,
That clothed with life, light, action, sweeps us on
Towards Beauty and Perfection, is no dream,—
Howe'er our weak conception bodies it!

(*A Messenger enters.*)

TIBERIUS.

Thou art from Capri, fellow! Are thy galleys,
That shall to-morrow bear us to our isle,
Safe anchored in the bay?

MESSENGER.

They wait the will
Of Cæsar;—if again he choose to tread
The spot that Jove has manifestly cursed.

TIBERIUS.

Ah, frightened knave! What say'st thou!

MESSENGER.

That which these eyes have seen. This morning, sir,
As our calmed vessels slowly float from shore,
The rock-girt island seemed to toss its bulk
Like our frail bark when winter's tempest blows.
Thy stony palaces were bent and swayed
Like the weak mast we govern. Then the tower,
Proud, lofty mass that frowns upon the deep,
Reeling from side to side, quivered and fell
In thunder on the beach!—A sudden breeze
Now rising from the south, swelled our dead sails,
And bore us trembling from this scene of havoc.

TIBERIUS.

Physician, hast thou ears—or are they fooled

Like eyes of mine! Frenzy, thy breath is on me!

Wine! wine there; bring it quickly! This grotesque
Fantastic fable should be quenched and drowned
With all the sable shapes that flock to it.

(*Ennia returns.*)

ENNIA (*apart to Caius*).

The wine is mixed by Macro—potently
To lull all pain asleep. I am enough
Fouled in your service, and will do no more.
Be thou the cup-bearer,—if yet thy will,
Uncancelled by remorse, thrust at his life.

CAIUS.

I have no fear to act the thing I think
Like whim-besotted women. Give it me!

Cæsar, the wine is craftily infused—
Thus spiced and freshly mingled, marvel not
That simple men in ecstasy supreme
Called him divine who gave it!

Ennia, see,

How eagerly he lifts it to his lips.

Soon are we safely anchored to that shore
That long has fled before our quickened hope.

CHARICLES

(advancing, takes the cup from Tiberius, and pours the wine upon the earth).

Give something to the gods! Thy guilty court
Dwelt not at Capri when its towers were razed!
One poor libation meanly pays such mercy!

TIBERIUS *(after a pause).*

There is but one of all this scented band
That durst so honor them. Yet heed thee, heed,
Lest thou presume too long on friendship past,
And one day bleed for like officiousness.

LUCULLUS.

The festal music that now rings within,
Calls Cæsar to the feast our hasting zeal
Has heaped to match his order.

TIBERIUS.

Life freshens at the sound, and the warmed heart
Leaps to the melody! Physician, come,

Pour thy libations to a mortal god
Whom it shall profit something. Have we garlands?

LUCULLUS.

This is the youth who bears them.

TIBERIUS.

Crown me, boy;
This yielding band of roses soothes the brow
That aches with costly metal!
Is the earth firm!—
Methought it shook and heaved but now like that
He told us of at Capri! Prodigy!
Ye all are stable, while I stagger here
As one who walks the galley's slippery deck,
When tempests lift our navies. To the feast—
We should reel after. Help me on, I say,
The will of Cæsar lives!—yet fitfully
It flashes:—Charicles—thy hand—thy hand—
How cold it seizes mine. Upon thy life
No word! on—on—Cæsar rules Cæsar still!

Lucullus, well this thirsty throng shall prove
The wine your jars have ripened; while our band

Of dancers and trained singers shall show thee
What gods we keep at Capri. Ha, our wreath
Has fallen—Bring another! Ennia,
The flush upon thy cheek rivals these flowers.
Our race, good Caius, ever won the smile
Of Roman beauty—thou art one of us!
The music quickens. Why stand prating here—
And let the ruddy moment of delight
Solicit us in vain! On to our revel!

[*Exeunt.*

The Act closes.

ACT II.

Ennia enters from the villa.

ENNIA.

A moment pour thy cooling breath, oh night,
Athwart my restless bosom. Ye cold stars,
Freeze up those quickened feelings which at times—
As even now they do—struggle beneath
The weight of years and folly. Should the heart
Still nourish its own venom—fret and waste
A languid being in the narrow path
Where custom binds it! No; though cramped by man,
Toyed, wheedled, slaved, at last we break the chain,
Renounce all mercy, tenderness, remorse,
And glut our starving passion. Let no dream
Of rest, revived affection, or of rays
Familiar hope once flickered, touch the soul
That fate sweeps on to power!—

Music again
Charges the air with pity;—mortal grief
Pours forth its plaint in harmonies of art,
Snatches the strolling breeze, and clogs its flight
Toned with a human sorrow. Hence! oh hence,
Thou language of the soul that mocks our life,
By rumoring a being all refined
From the dull dross that drags this feebleness,
Earthward from whence 'twas fashioned!
The young moon,
Bedded in fleecy vapor, streams repose
Vainly on this torn spirit. Glimmer on,
Thou passive, icy wonder, which our priests
Have mantled in a woman's fickleness!
Hadst thou the choler, rancor, spite, hate, love,
That ravens on her breast, thy drowsy beams
Would sparkle sharply through the scattered night,
And dumb with awe thy quaking worshippers.
Sea gust!—who sportest with the floating mists,
That heave and drift above me—lift my soul
To wander freely among airy things,
Grotesque imaginations, that may dull
This aching need of loving—born to crave,
Sting, perish, never to be satisfied!

Away thou life most false and incomplete!
Yearn, languish all my being! then create
Ideal nothings, worthy to provoke
Thy possible delirium of bliss,
The energy and madness of thy love.—
Flit then before me fair, absorbing shape
Wrapped in unearthly power,—let my life,
Spurning its selfish action, melt in thine
And quicken there to ripeness!
Loud debauch
Swells through the opening gates! Some parasites
Reel forth to chill their fever-whirling blood
From the cold breast of night! This wooded path
Shall shield me from their banter and light talk.

(As the doors of the villa open, a burst of revelry is heard. Then enter Charicles.)

CHARICLES.

Close up your doors again! Shut drunken mirth
And mad disorder in the tainted cell,
That dulls their guilty jangle to the ear
Of modest nature!—
Let me worship here.
The sainted benediction of the night

Floats softly through her temple. Every breath
Charged with the fragrance of the blooming earth,
Wafts absolution to the soul that feels
All error, foolishness, and doubt apart
From its true being. We do flaw ourselves,
So nobly fashioned, deeming we may not
Wipe out the stain our youthful wildness trucked
For pleasure coveted. We are not mocked,
Feeling that man must triumph over sense,
Which now he combats weakly. Aching, scarred
At every pore, the clay-enchanting life
Deserts the baffled soldier ; yet we know
Those thrusts and buffets that his dying arm
Drops feebly on his victor, still shall earn
A life immortal on the painted page,
That chronicles to the remotest time
The patriot's fruitless courage ! Oh thou god,
Or gods, or natural principle of right,
Which blindly we must worship !—shall we not
Receive again unmaimed the soul we lose,
Battling with evil that has vanquished us !

ENNIA (*coming forward*).

Does the physician, doubting his own art,

Beseech night's chilly finger to retard,
And time the throbbing of the hurried heart—
Even like an unskilled woman!

CHARICLES.

The live air
Pours subtler vigor through the healthy frame,
Than any draught wrung from the soothing weed,
Or quick'ning root, at bitter need expert
To minister to man.

ENNIA.

Your patient, sir—
Does he still suffer, play the boy, and mock
The hand that holds dominion in his grasp?

CHARICLES.

The frenzy of his revel ebbs; the eye,
That flashed with fearless lustre, dully falls
Upon the wanton throng. The lips that late
(So thou hast seen) flung sparks of ribald jest
On all that nature hallows, murmur now
And ooze a childish prattle. Caius Cæsar,
Silenced in wonder, gazes fearfully

Upon his sinking kinsman,—seeing well
The sudden culmination of his hope
Outstrip conspiracy and parricide.

ENNIA.

There is a mercy yet! The wretch shall die
By Heaven's stroke, not ours—Assurance blest,
I clasp thee! And perchance before the last,
His conscious mind may calmly designate
Our Caius his successor: then we rule
Untortured by the furies rumor feigns
Shall haunt usurpers.

CHARICLES.

It can hardly be
The mind shall so resume its healthy function,
As to prepare in calmness for an end,
That, recognized, must hurl the startled soul
Into chaotic torture. Memories past,
And images of terror, uncontrolled
By manly will, mingle with present things,
And in a sore perplexity of sense,
Crush out the feeble reason. Life will end
In a vague dream, unbroken into time,

While unconnectedly the avenging thoughts,
Draped all in ghastly horror, dimly flit
About the jaded brain. So far as art
Foretells what shall be, by experience
Of what has been, thus shall the monarch die.

ENNIA.

And thus we climb to power;—power, that will make
Our lives decay as his! So we still pant
For an ideal existence, to supply
The stimulus to being, which we crave
To thrust us from this passionless routine
Of present meanness, folly, and contempt
At the poor show we witness. The fooled soul
Must struggle on,—not turn upon itself
In sickening revolution. Oh sir, say—
For from thy presence seems to flow a charm
That wrests the question from me—is there not
Some cunning trick to turn to harmony
The discords, harsh and clashing, that repel
The love, the peace we covet?

CHARICLES.

We are not left

To totter down to death, swayed to and fro
By every breath of passion. Mastership
Of our own thought, won and preserved
Through effort, shall invest the craving mind
With calmness; but this faculty divine
Comes slow and rarely to our fickle race.
Yet those there are, who can the will command,
Banish the frivolous degrading doubt,
And singly turn the workings of the soul
To one great object. Such a quality
Is priest and sovereign unto him who holds it.

ENNIA.

I recognize a wisdom in thy words
That we can never reach. To know a peace
Beyond, above us, is the misery
That mocks our impotence! Art thou a man
So wrapt and crusted in with smoky dreams,
That no conception of a happiness,
Not won but hourly grasped at, goads thy soul?

CHARICLES.

Strength to conceive the thing we may not gain
Shall bless or curse us, at our proper choice.

To strive for good,—not to abide in good,
Is destiny most noble. We are palled
In our vexed youth to find the thing we love
Melt from our grasp;—then, waking, we perceive
That the hot hope that struggled in the mind
Repelled the sober blessing nature pours
Most tenderly on all. Bosomed in peace,
We prison our own souls, and torture them
With petty toys Fate dances in the air,
Which touched, must fade and turn to bitterness.

(*Enter Caius Cæsar.*)

CAIUS.

Physician, thou hast saved us! and shalt tell
The doubting world Tiberius died untouched
By mortal instrument. He labors now,
And fights off death but feebly; and we hope
Before the last, he shall be urged to name
Ourselves to take the throne. Our title then
Cannot be shaken. I withdraw awhile,
Lest some should say through tricking, and by fright,
I wrung the crown from him:—but go thou in,
To witness what my zealous partisans
Shall plague him into uttering. Men will deem

Thy evidence unpurchased. Tarry not—
Know it shall profit all.

CHARICLES.

I am obedient.

ENNIA.

How meekly our sage scholar bows his head
To win the smile of Power! His plans, most noble—
But their expression in the life, how mean!—
Nay pardon, Charicles, my shrewish tongue
Libelled the heart most foully;—thou art not
Wrenched from thy course by interest or threat;
But envying thee too much, I seize suspicion,
And doubting thee, loathe less my tarnished self.

CHARICLES.

I go to hush the brawling company,
Who siege the bloated fragment of a man,
That I have once called friend. Humanity
Shall not be wholly driven from the wretch,
Who lingers there, self-filed and desolate!

[*Charicles returns to the villa.*

CAIUS.

Answer him not! Check not his shallow whims,—
For now I prize his presence, who shall give
The people surety that the steps I mount,
Are spotted not by blood.

ENNIA.

Art thou secure
If he names no successor,—or another?

CAIUS.

'Tis but a new assurance that I seek
Of what is now most certain. Grant he dies
Not naming me his heir—then I shall rise
By clamor of the army, and paid throats
Of vassal senators—paid to pretend
A general call to power;—yet the sway
Yielded by act of his I doubly gripe,
And dare the gods to cast me!

ENNIA.

Yet 'tis strange,
How in the presence of this Charicles,

Our plotted height of power crumbles to meanness.
These eager hopes in vapid languor die,
And my soul feels the weary ache of climbing.

CAIUS.

Look on me then, and shelter here thy weakness.
Think when thy hand shall wield imperial sway,
When from thine eye, power, like its beauty, flashes,—
How thou mayst burn, ay, brand with usury,
Into the hearts of certain jealous matrons,
Old scorn and spite!

ENNIA.

There, thou hast made me strong!
My sinking nerve is fed, and I am thine.

(*Enter Lucullus, followed by attendants bearing torches.*)

CAIUS.

Why do these torches taint the wholesome air
With their thick smoke?

LUCULLUS.

The Emperor orders it;

For he would drink the wandering breeze of night,
Yet cannot brook the darkness.

CAIUS.

Hath he waked
From that dull stupor which we thought the chill
Of instant death? Hath he named no successor?

LUCULLUS.

None, sir. His sinews tough, tho' wrenched and torn
By mortal agony, cord in the soul.
When some essayed to take the signet ring,
The type of all his power, feigning his words
Had bid thee wear it,—lo! a sudden strength
Poured through the dying frame; up, up, he sprang,
With furious gesture cowed the cringing throng,
And gasped for the physician. Charicles,
Even at the instant entering, caught the moan,
And hurried to his side. Then self-abandoned,
The dotard clove to him as child to nurse,
And bade him quench the ceaseless fire that scorched
The citadel of life.

CAIUS.

Then Charicles
Would damp this heated reveller in the dew,
That chills our festal garments ?

LUCULLUS.

Craving strong
For the free air Tiberius uttered oft,
Ere the physician yielded to his prayer
A slow concession. Then the fear of darkness
O'erwhelmed him, and these torch-bearers are sent
To temper the obscurity he dreads.

(*Tiberius, supported by attendants, enters. Charicles follows.*)

TIBERIUS.

Ay, here I breathe more freely ; and these throbs,
That beat so heavily the spirit out,
Are timed to slower measure : I had pressed
The bound extreme, where human misery
Tears out a passage through her prison house,
And mingles with the ether ; but this blast
Kindles the life within me ; I rule still !

CAIUS.

Are you not weary, uncle? The gray haze
Of morning glimmered on the distant hills,
Ere your red torches gave the world new darkness.

TIBERIUS.

Weary? no, no! I'm fresh and strong, good Caius,
And can outfeast the maddest of you all!
Ay, bout and brawl with any curly youth,
High-flushed with nimble Bacchus!
                    Take away
These flowers;—freshened by the dew-fraught air,
Their odor sickens me. Nay, Charicles,
Come closer—leave me not—for I would drain
A portion of thy calmness. Dreams of horror,
And fears unutterable fix their clutch
Here, here, even in the heart! Lo! I may not,—
I cannot grapple with their thronging host!

CAIUS.

Mark you, Lucullus, how he mumbles there,
And whispers the physician. The thick words,
That quiver from his lips, break on my ear

In music; murmuring, another hour
Shall seat me monarch!—
Have the messengers
Sent by the senate yet arrived to greet us?
One of our servants passed them on the road,
And warned their speedy coming. Do the lights
That flash and hurry through the court below
Announce their presence?

LUCULLUS.

Some unwonted stir
Troubles the night;—no other cause can bring it.

CAIUS.

Come, we will meet this mission; for to bend
Most humbly to these reverent senators,
And their unwashed supporters, is our part,—
At least to-day:—to-morrow!—Well, no boasts.
Come, Ennia, show these vassals what an eye,
And regal brow, shall dignify their crown!
Then follow, friends, and lift your voices up
In sudden acclamation, when they say
The senate have preferred me. Bring your torches,—
For he can die by moonlight. After us—all!

(*Caius Cæsar descends the hill, followed by all but Tiberius and Charicles.*)

TIBERIUS.

Let me lie here. Carpet the chilly earth
With your thick cloaks; so, I am patient now.
Why is this bustle? The black breath of night
Is heavy on us yet:—I must depart
At sunrise, and ere night we shall carouse
At Capri. Ha! why go these lights from us?

CHARICLES.

See where the moon rolls back the draping cloud,
To bathe in modest splendor every leaf,
That flutters drowsy whispers to the breeze.
We want no torches;—let them go unquestioned.

TIBERIUS.

Nay, I cannot support the maze of fiends
That mock me with their laughter! Bid them return,
And let their tapers scare these busy thoughts
That thicken in the darkness,—for their light,
Warm with domestic memories, should quench out
These shapes projected from the sable night

In livid streaks of fire! Yet 'tis most strange,
This potent fever, which doth shrivel up
My very life, ay, scalds each separate vein,
May not blaze forth, and lighting all the world,
Beacon our race from whelming misery.

CHARICLES.

Look up, old man, and with an effort cast
Thy soul upon the universe. Implore
The peace that rained upon thy boyish head,
When, all untented, thou didst purely share
The spacious couch of nature. For those orbs,
Whose daily changes, so the learned dream,
Direct our lives, stream something of their power,
To bear above the feeble aches of earth
Their trusting worshippers.

TIBERIUS.

Weak, weak, and bound
So strongly to its loathsome dwelling here,
The spirit may not mount. The light that streams
E'en through these darkened portals of the brain,
Withers the feeble remnant of a life
That lurks about me. Mutter not of peace;

The very word bruited upon the night
Scalds the dry lip it passes. Think of him,
God Hercules, whom the grief-painting Greek
Gave mighty verse to blazon forth all pain,
That could be fixed in language! Dost thou not
Recall that misery intrenched in speech!—
The virgin-chorus of immortal pity!—
Are they not vivid still?

CHARICLES.

Faintly they show;
For cares and busy years despoil the mind
Of its best treasures.

TIBERIUS.

Yet those verses now
Blossom afresh within me, and my grief—
All that is physical—outwells in words,
That utter the extremity of ill
Our shrinking frame can suffer! But, oh here!
Here, in the centre, grows an agony
That mocks expression:—Thou life-blighting pest—
Immedicable thought! thy potent fangs,
Fleshed deep into the being, rankle on,

And taint with blackest pestilence the blood,
That trickles through the heart. Oh Charicles,
Drug, poison, kill, this wolfish Memory,
That from vacuity coins wretchedness!

Why are these voices? Why went Caius Cæsar
So suddenly from hence?

CHARICLES.

The senate, sir,
Send, of their gravest members, certain men
To hail an emperor, and confer with him,
Touching oppression and high-handed wrong,
That crimson all the country.

TIBERIUS.

Let them chafe
In their own capitol! Ill-timed this visit:
We have no mind to hear their stale complaint.
They shall partake the doom Procillius knew,
He and his brother rebels, who would thrust
Petitions in our face:—Now strongly gyved,
In Roman dungeons they wear out their lives!

But why went Caius to them? He will not
Cringe, twist, and stoop before these reckless dolts.
I know him, subtle, crafty, troublesome,
To commoners; but *I* have raised him up,
And, bounteous in my largess, steeped his youth
In every riot and voluptuous joy
That sense can hanker for. Peevish restraint
Harassed his frolics never: he partook
Each melting madness hot-lipped Pleasure flung
About our island! He is bound to me
By every chain that patronage and gifts
Can rivet on the man fed by their bounty!

They climb the hill—A throng of men I see,
But none distinctively. Are these the fools
Who so desire to belch their petty griefs,
That they must steal unbidden to my presence,
And after bleed for it? Well, let them come!—
And yet this crowd strikes marvel to my soul—
Death! Are those guards of mine, who cheer the traitors?
Where's Caius Cæsar?

CHARICLES.

At the head he walks,

Clasping the hand of one, whose dignity
Acknowledged by the rest, proclaims him chief
And spokesman of this mission.

TIBERIUS.

Traitor ! Ha—
Blast the suspicion ! Let me up, I say,
For I am young and supple ! Does he dare—
Or do these clamors thrilling in my ears
Cheat my eyes also !

(*Enter Caius Cæsar, Lucullus, guards, Messengers, and others.*)

Well, what means this throng—
Who are these base intruders ? Answer me,—
Or I shall grow and blaze before your sight,
Yea, rain down fire upon ye, that shall singe
With torture exquisite the very breath
That pants your stale complaining ! Answer me.

CAIUS (*aside to his party*).

Be patient, friends. This burst of dying rant
Shall harm you nothing—see, he reels and staggers,
Grasping his servants for support ! Again
If he demand your business, hide it not.

TIBERIUS.

Speak, Caius! lest the rage that fills me here,
Break through the mesh of doubt, and marshal thee
The way Procillius and his comrades went,
To clank out treason to the sunless vault,
That tombs their wretchedness.

CAIUS.

Pray you look there!—
Come from the throng, Procillius! follow ye,
Whom the just senate frees from base restraint,
And honors as the country's patriots!
You threat me with their company,—I claim it!

TIBERIUS.

Is this a dream firm-frozen in the brain,
That flies not with its ghastly comrades? Hence,
Hence, hideous fantasy!
Caius, these fiends,
Whom here thou seest so thickly grouped about,
Feign treachery in thee—in thee, who knew
E'en in thy freshest youth each quaint device,
That goaded luxury could think;—each subtle tinge

Long-wantoned fancy could to pleasure add
Was lavished at thy word! Ingratitude,
Nay, black rebellion, to thy king and patron—
Fie! 'tis too monstrous! Make a lesser lie,
Ye torturing powers, for this too gross deceit
Bounds harmless from me!

MESSENGER.

Listen then to those
Sent by the senate, to declare the will
Of Romans, too long crushed beneath the rule
Of thy curst monarchy. Though gored and torn
By foul oppression, Rome has found the strength
To curb thy dying havoc. She defies
The carnage-craving dotard, stung to death
With his own infamies. The noble men,
Condemned to waste in dungeons, walk our streets,
Freed by the senate; and, by them despatched,
We linger here till the quick hours shall give
Our state a better ruler;—till we shout,
Long reign Caligula the emperor!

TIBERIUS.

Delusions fall from me, and fancies melt

To bitter truth. Shiver these senators,
Ye direful pains, more cruel than man's wrath
Can heap upon his fellow! lo, I claim
Your seething ministry to scorch these knaves!
Wrench ye and twist the cords that bind their souls
In mortal agony—but break no thread!
Make them groan out eternity in minutes,
Trail their foul bodies through the jeering world,—
Rend, shatter, mangle them, that they may know
A little half of what Tiberius feels,
And he shall cry you, *cease!*—glutted and drunk
With satisfaction.

Oh, I faint again!
Where is Procillius! Softly—let me lie
Here, on the cold wet earth! Oh, Charicles,
Wring from the brain these bitter memories,
From the hot heart draw out this latest grief,
Though the life follow it.

CHARICLES.

Conceive these plagues
But earth-born fantasies, alike unreal,
Alike all impotent to grieve or touch
The manliest part of life.

Throw thy mind upward to the fresh'ning dawn;
Mark where the poet Phœbus doth again
Write his rich fancies on the glowing mists,
That drape his eastern chamber!
How like a lover every burnished rack
Drinks his young inspiration! till informed
And filled with music, the thick harmonies
Gush forth to charm our world with prophecy
Of her lord's coming.
Listen! the touch of morning on the plain,
Makes every tree a lyre: Lo, how it sends
A soothing energy through every vein,
And pours abundance into weed and leaf,
Through measureless creation! E'en to die—
Once more to mix with the creative stream,
That bounds exultant in the waking brute,
Blooms in the flower, and bursting grandly on
Through heaven's high chamber hurls the blazing globes,
Twinkled in pallid clusters down to earth
To blend our fluttering, uncertain thought
With passionless eternity—to die—
To breathe in simple confidence the soul
Forth to embrace the morning—were but sweet
At such an hour as this!

TIBERIUS.

Tangled in snares—
With nimble torments rent—
What words can goad the fancy to depart
From the vexed bulk that holds it! I have dwelt,
Ay, wrestled daily, with such mighty throes,
As treble singly the extremest plunge
Of man's conception. I am Cæsar yet!
Away, and let me up! for I am strong,
Strong, to chastise these traitors. Though the breath
Shall hoarsely rattle in the gasping throat—
Though the thick words shall heavily presage
The cheerless end of nature—though the dawn
Scowls on me—I am strong!—and do defy
This rebel senate! Seize this crazy wretch,
And his crime-clotted comrades. Come, despatch,
Then on to Capri! There we do contemn
Your saucy insurrection. Pent and walled
In our strong island, we do hold your threats
A theme for laughter merely. Barriers
Shall there defend our frolics, while we send
Armies to crush and scourge these carping dolts
Into submission. Come, despatch, I say!

These guards move slowly! Are they still ungyved?
I cannot see them plainly—Charicles—
Be near me still—ay, let me clutch this sword,
For we can fight our younger battles o'er
If need shall be! Now lead me to the house.
Arouse our servants! All the galleys wait.
Nay, bustle here, come—come.—Away for Capri!

(*Tiberius, supported by Charicles and attendants, is led into the villa.*)

The Act closes.

ACT III.

Caius Cæsar, Ennia.

CAIUS.

We have attained the summit! All the guards
Have softly echoed the great cry for us,
Which we have wrung from Rome. Their voices wait
The speedy word that shall announce his death,
To cleave the air with clamor! We may breathe
And bask our languid person in the sun:—
A little moment more shall seat thee empress,—
Reality absorbs thy haunting hope,—
And thou canst envy no one!

ENNIA.

Baseless vaunt!
Can any gaudy pomp of royalty,
Or costly harness, which the state binds on
To those who rule it, satisfy the soul

That restless dwells within us! Hope fulfilled
Is but a dream and fable!

CAIUS.

Yet the truth
Now spurns thy doubting! See these friends appear,
Hasting to tell the best.

(Enter Crassus and Lucullus.)

What am I now?

CRASSUS.

The Emperor!

LUCULLUS.

Caligula, the lord
Of Rome, and father of her people, hail!

CAIUS.

Ha, I have grown;—but not above the friends
Who were the first to greet me. Well, how died
The terror-stricken tyrant?

CRASSUS.

In a swoon
He faded from the earth; upon his vexed

And tortured life, the dreaded shade of death
Descended suddenly. His guilty soul,
Quite vanquished with its griefs, so faintly passed,
We might not mark the moment. Now his trunk,
Stretched pale and lifeless in the hall within,
Is food for mockery and bitter gibes,
To the poor knaves he lorded.

CAIUS.

It is well.
Did Macro snatch the state-conferring ring
And purple mantle from him? These must show,
And instantly, on his successor—yet—
Yet I am loth to take them from the body.

LUCULLUS.

They are stripped from him. Macro rent them off,
Crying their richness and authority
Befit a better ruler!

CAIUS.

Orders were
To do e'en thus—he is a friend most faithful!—
Lucullus, we go in to deck ourselves

In these god-given trappings. But speed thou,
Who here art master, to the court below,
Where all the guards are quartered, where a throng,
Drawn from the neighboring country, press and flock
About this reverent mission—quick to hear
How beats the city's pulse. At once proclaim
The tyrant's death—and having wasted time
In question and reply, (for we must robe
To play the regal part,) lead to this place
All who may hear thy voice! Thou hast received
The Emperor's orders.

LUCULLUS.

To fulfil them all.

[*Exit.*

CAIUS.

Go thou before me, Crassus; I would not
Approach him suddenly. Call Charicles—
Nay, he is here already. We have need
Of one the people trust,—he must remain
Till we are strongly fixed.

(*Enter Charicles.*)

Receive our welcome!
Although we rise like yonder sun in power,

Like him we throw our benefits to all,
To thee as to the others! Stay awhile;
For having seen, ay, and foretold as well,
This death that is our life—the peevish tongue
Of scandal cannot touch us. Crassus, come,
Lead us where lies the decorated scarf
Of our new state! We must return a monarch!
[*Exeunt Caius Cæsar and Crassus.*

CHARICLES.

Does the intrepid consort share the joy,
That she has toiled to compass?

ENNIA.

Joy!—alas,
The very word doth shrivel on the lip.
Well, well thou know'st how empty is the thing
That we have gained—or seized most shamelessly.
Are we not limited and hedged about
When most our schemes have prospered? Screened from us
By the black veil that curtains time to come,
Lingers our best of life. A jealous hope,
Crushed love, and honor lost forever, prey

Upon us. Canst thou understand the pang
Of passions disappointed—canst thou dream
All that a woman knows, who bears a heart
More finely touched and delicately wrought,
Than those who herd about her! No, alas!
Thy stern and healthy holiness of soul
Can never paint the weary thing it is,
When the blythe hope and confidence of youth,
Drain drop by drop away. This intellect
Outgrows your mock religions. Then to see
What toys we are to men—to be deceived,
Cajoled by promises, enslaved, betrayed,
By flattery insulted!—this, ay this,
Is woman's happiest state. Unrecognized
Her life's young fervor, and her sympathies
Keen, eager, sparkling with the freshest tide
Poured from the cup of nature, are repelled
And stagnate into silliness or crime,
As she is crushed,—or, burning into power,
Crushes her wronger!

CHARICLES.

Woman, I perceive
Through all these bitter words a spot in thee,

That the gross clasp of flattery hath not touched.
Oh could it be, the fatal seal that hangs
Above this future greatness, might not fall
To stamp it into being—there were hope;—
But now, I fear the breath that feebly plays
In yon deserted chamber, will quench out
Thy best of life in parting!

ENNIA.

Hopes or prayers
Alike are worthless; for this blotted life
Hath passed already; and our Caius stands
Supreme and perfect master over thee,
As over all below us.

CHARICLES.

No, not yet:—
For know the semblance of that certainty
That seats Caligula is counterfeit;—
And Caius, like a tinselled player struts,
To ape the monarch merely.

ENNIA.

Ha, deceived!

Dwells yet about his heart the little heat
That makes and unmakes men! Are we then mocked,
Fooled, fooled, unto the last! But 'tis not so—
Or Charicles were near his wretched charge.

CHARICLES.

'Twere madness now; else would the curious crowd
Press busily about him, and wrench out
The life that loiters faintly. I must seem
Deluded as the rest, who parted straight
From the spoiled body. Yet a trusted slave,
Obedient to my order, waits beside
This friend-abandoned couch, and cherishes
The slow returning life.

ENNIA.

Tell Caius not
What shadows dress his person, when he comes
To take the people's homage; or his hand,
Bloodied enough already, shall dispatch
This new created phantom!

CHARICLES.

'Twere the same

To him, who ever shall be shadow-cloaked
Nor guess the coarse delusion; but to thee,
In whom I note that vivid restless eye
That looks beyond the present, this weak show
Shall never harden to reality.
Then let it fall away—and go thou forth
Purged and regenerate. Nerve thy saddened soul
To put away these empty fantasies,
That trick thee on to ruin. Know, thy will,
Steeled first in self-denial, may dispel
These baffling doubts that jeopard all thyself!

ENNIA.

It is too late!—I know not how to cringe
Before the god your cunning fellows feign
To patron trampled woman. For there are
Enough, too many, faint and weary souls,
Whom you can hold degraded and content,
Tickled to mumm and mumble off their strength,
As the sleek priest directs. My spirit spurns
This refuge men have built us, and I stand
Erect to suffer—to despair, perchance—
But proud to hold reason unravished still!

CHARICLES.

Thou hast not found the mission of those lives,
That swell with power forever barred from action.
'Tis hard, most hard to learn; for we do strive,
Ay, madly throe and grapple with our fate,
Too blind to grasp the sober recompense,
That compensating nature ever pours
Where she has much denied. The destiny
Of a proud woman—who hath soul and mind
Too large to fill with priestly mockeries,
Which are, and ever will be, man's device
To busy and to rule her—though it seem
Most bitter, may beget a sober joy
Unimaged to the worldling. Battle not
With thy restricted fate; but gently yield
To what has been ordained. Thou hast no room,
Rightly to show the genius and the strength
That riot hot within thee! Some may not
Spin out their schemes for trapping to themselves
The glossy reek of flattery, that shall taint
Those who most fairly win it. Then pass out
Into the world about us;—let this sun,
Streamed through the opened portals of the sense,

Caress and ripen all thy sullen mind.
'Tis only when ambition's galling spur,
Bound in by cords thick-twisted through the heart,
Is by long sufferance dulled and deadened out,
That we receive existence, and therein
Do learn to triumph nobly. Our despair
Falls as a mantle as we leave the broil
For the world's painted honors, and receive
From nature and ourselves the strength that brings
A perfect consolation. Ennia,
I speak no foolish theories; but have lived—
And learnt most bitterly the truth I utter.
Hear me! nor weakly cast away thyself,
That may be saved—still saved—from wretchedness!

ENNIA.

It is too late—too late:—A woman's life
Hath regular degrees to climb or fall,
And as we press on each, the former sinks
Behind us. We can never pause or turn—
Fate whips us sternly on! Yet sir, believe,
Could I have felt thy presence ere I stood
Before the golden gates of womanhood,

I had received these gifts of form and strength,
To cast aside fragrant with purer use.

(Re-enter Caius Cæsar, followed by Crassus and attendants.)

CAIUS.

Are we too soon arrived! Our court and guards,
Are they not here to greet us?

CRASSUS.

Nay, they climb
In glittering mass to hail thee, see, they toil
And labor to the summit. Now they catch
Thy regal robe flash welcome in the sun!
Lucullus waves his hand—what shouts are those
That answer! All their caps leap to the air,
And hark!—they cry—"The god Caligula!"

CAIUS.

The god Caligula! Physician, see
Where now I stand to shame thy medicines!
Unless thy skill find quick'ning for the dead,
As physic for the living, I am firm.
The bond is broke that held thy mumbling lord

Before the place I craved. This jocund crowd
Takes little thought of that gaunt spectacle,
That coldly presses the wine-spotted stones.
What is the profit of thine honesty—
Thrust quite aside, unrecognized, displaced
Before this sweeping surge of sycophants!

CHARICLES.

We toil to be forgotten; and at night
Unnoticed sink to silence. 'Tis decreed.
The sober daily duties of men's lives
Win from the world no statues. Yet a tone
Worthy the chords celestial that are placed
Harmonious in our grasp, shall ripple on
And softly range the ages. We must toil
To be forgotten; yet not so the good
Or ill our life shall furnish. That impressed
On those around us, and by them bequeathed
To all who follow after, hurtles still
Through the world's heart of being: therein lies
Our certain immortality. Reflect,
Thou future monarch! dare not trifle now,—
For every act of thine peals far and wide,
Its proper note of shame or blessedness.

CAIUS.

We ask nor drug nor counsel; thou art kept
To tell this crowd our uncle was consumed
By his own foul diseases, not dispatched
By rumored treason. This thy work! 'Tis mine,
To greet these heralds of my dignity.

(Enter Lucullus, followed by a crowd of guards, citizens, &c.)

LUCULLUS.

Brothers and soldiers, freed from bloody bondage
Beneath a tyrannous and galling yoke,
Lift up your voices—give the heaven your caps—
Cry, Hail Caligula the Emperor!

(A great clamor.)

CAIUS.

For this most fresh and cheering welcome, thanks.
Know we stand here untarnished;—The grey wretch,
Abhorred by Heaven, by Heaven has been dethroned.
Our hands are bloodless;—and for proof we bring
This grave physician. Charicles, declare
Tiberius' death, and how our spotless self

Stayed not his breath from lingering to this hour,—
Our wish and effort were that he should live.

CHARICLES.

That wish is granted! Bend thine eyes but there,
Nay, 'tis no apparition! Lift again
Your pliant voices—See, how strong he walks!
Shout welcome to the god Tiberius!

[*As Charicles speaks, the doors of the villa open and discover Tiberius stripped of his royal garments. He breaks from an attendant who supports him, and comes forward.*]

TIBERIUS.

Palsy these limbs—numb every nerve in death—
The stifling fury waked by such revolt
Would vent itself through bones that had bleached out
A century in the sun! Then let me grow
And tower in my wrath until I swell
To bulk tremendous, and so toppling down
Crush out this league of robbers!—
Caius Cæsar,
Have I not fed thy gross and lawless youth
With license that is proverbed! Must I whine

And crouch to thee for leave to die—to die,
As peacefully as dog or slave, unracked
Save by the easy wrenches of decay—
Not gored and galled by black ingratitude
Of a pride-bloated kinsman! Dost thou hear
These jangling words denounce thee? Seize him, slaves!
Bind fast this puppet monarch!—nay, keep place,
I, who have wrestled with such ghastly throes
As would have parched an army into dust,
Can blight him singly! Ha—now—now,—he melts
And shrivels at my breath—scorched in the blaze,
That bursts about my veins, he wails for mercy
Ay, clench thy teeth! Pray for thy life to crack!
We two shall seethe in agony forever—
Oh satisfaction! bitter and most blest!—

CAIUS.

Appalling sight! Keep this crazed babbler from me!
I charge ye, drag him hence;—for though as mortal
A terror steals upon me, and I shake
At this enormous prodigy—yet ye,
On whom the deadly flashings of his eye
Are not so thickly poured, may drive away
This spectre, ay, and stifle out the voice

That growls these curses on the dizzy head,
Crowned by your acclamation.

LUCULLUS.

Friends, arise,
It is too late to turn. Come press we on,
And in a mass bear this sick tyrant back
Into the hall. The morning sky affords
A roof too fair for one distempered thus!
Your voices given, there is no room for choice—
Obey the Emperor proclaimed but now!
Clear were his words! Off with Tiberius!

[*A great confusion. Tiberius is seized and borne into the villa. Lucullus and Crassus follow hastily, and after them Charicles.*]

ENNIA.

So thou hast gained the summit of all hope,
And leav'st ambition, and that gnawing ache
After the unattainable, that marks
The brow, and wrinkles up the soul, far, far
In the hot plain below! Incautious man!
Thy empty boast still frights the laughing breeze,
Thy regal stride streaked in the passing mist,

Still throws fantastic shadows! Strive again,
Again, adore some phantom of the mind,
By fancy changed to an external thing,
That lives in thy hereafter!

CAIUS.

Woman, cease—
This is no time for mocking. We have gauged
Our bliss too soon; for it should seem there dwells
A power beyond us, whose behest can change
Our certainties to dreams and emptiness.

ENNIA.

Then pause to ponder wisely; nor despise
This scathed and blighted warning of a fate,
That lurks with horror to crush out the reign,
Blood-stained and monstrous in its infamy.
And let that spark of highest life to man,
That hid by bestial riot and debauch,
Still frets and festers in us, kindle up
And light thee from the curses of a world!

CAIUS.

Peace, woman! what we learn by prodigies,

That plant their lessons in the living eye,
Words but dilute and weaken. We are taught
By hard experience, as the chafing tide
Smooths the rough pebble to a polished gem.
Our policy, when once the height is gained,
Shall work reforms most needed, and restrain
This court of sottish brawlers; for I quail
At thought of end so black and direful.

ENNIA.

Build thus thy safety, Caius; for we know
In the hot chase for luring dignities,
Ambition cannot bend to study form,—
But bubbles onward, as the nimble brook
Leaps by the flowers that fringe its sedgy bed,
And hurries reckless to the sea—to find
The waters salt and bitter, that from far
Glanced merrily, and beckoned to the hills.
Oh, keep about thee better friends than those,
Who now in bloody passion seek the life,
That nourished all their rankness!

CAIUS.

Nay, these men

Do patriots solemn work, and recompense
Rich and abundant—rarely patriots' pay—
Shall line their chests with silver. Yet I keep,
If princely favors are not powerless,
This calm physician;—for 'tis wise to trust
A royal life to hands unparched by bribes.
Hark! how the growing tumult swells within
And breathes a tone of triumph! No dismay
Again shall wrinkle the new day in horror!

(Lucullus, Crassus, and Charicles enter. The crowd follow in confusion. Among them are those bearing the body of Tiberius, which is cast upon the earth.)

LUCULLUS.

Again we do salute Caligula!
There lies this pampered and remorseless man,
The wreck and ghastly refuse of misrule!
The flaming lights of lust and cruelty,
Have one by one gone out. The dazzling beam
Of mid-day cannot tinge his night to show
How dead the darkness lies. Come and behold,—
At length this mockery of humanity
Hath wearied out his scourgers.

CRASSUS.

And again,
Caligula, we hail thee sovereign,
And ruler of this empire; and we pray,—
That schooled by this black pageantry of death
Ignoble and unpitied,—our new lord
Will tender well the fabric he sustains,
And purge this Asiatic luxury
From court and state, before it crushes out
Our ancient manhood, and that hardiness
Wherewith the past frowns on us.

CAIUS.

But we doubt
Our right to rule e'en now. Physician, say
Is he yet past reviving?—if it be
He cannot wake to curse me, why, I take
The title you have offered, and shall build
With moderation, and determined zeal
The state you bid me govern. Yet declare
If dead Tiberius be! speak, Charicles,
For on thy word, still shackled to the truth,
My soul shall float to empire.

CHARICLES.

Govern then
In quiet awe; feeling the weighty trust
This hour bestows. Tiberius hath lost
His lease of black oppression: speak we not
Of his disgraces further. How he died
I may not wholly answer; for the crowd
Thronged thick about the bed, and only swayed
As something heaved and struggled in the midst,
More and more feeble grew the frequent throes,
Till suddenly a stillness fell on all,
And then the muffled mystery of death
Shuddered along the chamber! From the face,
When Macro first uncovered its fixed lines,
The startled crowd retreated,—and I saw
Caligula was monarch. If a doubt
Still linger, lift that mantle from the brow
It covers. Thou shalt find a surer proof
Of thy high place, than human breath can utter.

CAIUS.

No let it lie: I will not look again
Upon this stainer of our race and honor,

This Cæsar but in title, unallied
Unto the blood of Julius. 'Tis declared
That jealous zeal shall build again our state,
To simple firmness and contented strength.
And ye, whose clamors thrust us where we stand,
Be near our person, where your fervent cares
Shall win advantage. Crassus and Lucullus,
Friends both, are not forgotten ;—nay another,
By liberal favor, shall retain the place—
That he has filled most faithfully and well :
Know, Charicles, our bounty bids thee wait
About us as physician, to protect
Our life; as thou hast shielded that he bore,
Who was thy friend and master.

CHARICLES.

Pardon, sir ;
The intervention of a solemn calm
Between repose and action, rounds the life
That nature offers man—and no light cause
Should break this interval. I sought this court,
That tender skill of old companionship
Might somewhat soothe the anguish of a wretch,
Abandoned to the plots and mockeries,

Of those who shared his loathsome revelries,
And to the scorn of all. Look ! he has passed
His retribution—I am needed not.
In private quiet let me linger out
A few short days ere my release shall come.
For even now impressions, newly faint,
Dislimn and vanish, and before the dawn
The consciousness bounds into action—quick
By instinct to devote to life the hours
That hurry through the closing gates of Time.

CAIUS.

Depart then at thy pleasure ! 'Twas our wish
To cheer with profit, and society,
The desolation, doubts, and thick'ning pains
Which are the legacy that Age receives
To sting him bitterly to craving death.
But since alone, inactive for the world,
Thou would'st wear out the remnants of the mind—
So shall it be—depart in peace and safety.

CHARICLES.

Age is not desolate : our memory
Concentrates on the flash of happiness,

That has shot by us, and in mercy leaves
All else to night, and silence. The serene,
Pale twilight, vespered by soft-flowing notes,
That hail the parting of the garish day,
Melts lovingly to darkness: so the mind,
That feeds itself with labor, and retains
In wholesome discipline its tenement,
Shall fade most tranquilly to pleasant rest.
Uncramped by pain,—uncrutched by doltish creed,—
Nature invites the weary to lie down,
To rest and live at once;—to rest the thought—
To charm these jaded pulses of the brain,—
To dull the face, that burning through long nights,
Mocks the dark void that shattered love has left;—
And yet to live in pure and passive life,—
To harp the tempest in the vocal oak,
To gaze undazzled at the face of day
In the light-craving blossom,—or refined
To airy vapor, drink the sunset in,
And rain its golden glories down to men
In liberal profusion. To the soul
Uncloyed by narrow fable, unensnared
By the foul grasp of passion, this, the end
Of nature, is her favor last and best.

ENNIA.

And is this all! thou, who hast studied oft
The final shudder or the rarer smile,
As through the languid limbs oblivion
Diffuses its repose—has nothing flashed
To light that grand conception of our race,
Which builds up temples and inspires song?
Shall we not think this consciousness hath life,
Distinct from form and fabric, and may rise
An exhalation, viewless near the earth,
But thick'ning to a shape, as drifting on
Through thinner air, it basks in light unshrouded!

CHARICLES.

Nay! this majestic possibility—
The phantom that the fervid blood of youth
Imbues with life, or grasping superstition
Fevers for selfish profit—manly thought
Fails to redeem from shadow. Our research
Sees how the soul elaborates itself
From the coarse nurture that supplies the frame,
With means to grow and perish; and we mark
How they are one, together. We observe

A morsel undemanded to repair
The wastes of daily use, or an excess
In pleasure or in toil, unseat your gods
And fashion new religions—shrivel up
In frowns and cruelty the face of Jove,
Zeus, Apis, Belus,—or what other name
Man gives the deity diseases make
Of that, for which his art can find no shape,
His language no expression adequate.
Then blemish not thy future, that shall change
As damps, or study, or enfeebling lusts
Mope in the wearied brain ;—but calmly deem
Perfection is before us, clearly glassed
In each pure fancy that the heart conceives,
Yet feels too noble for the wavering will
To strike into existence.—Our best life
Breaks from the present, and flows strongly on
To chafe and fret the barrier, that fate
Builds round our little knowledge. It may be
The glowing particle that wields thine arm,
That loves and suffers through these instruments,
Shall learn to cast them,—and yet bear and know.
Or it may be this chance-commingled mass
Of energy and weakness, shall dissolve,

Again to mix with less impurity
In other life, built on the best of thine.
And thus, still changing, purifying still,
All that is guiltless in thy life shall live—
Pervading time—coursing its stream forever!

CAIUS.

Farewell physician! We respect thy wish—
Depart with honorable furtherance.
But let the rest now follow us within:
There shall our plans be faithfully unrolled
How best to use your gift; for know ye all—
Since fate that dallied with our expectation
Hath lifted us to place—we shall rebuke,
By clemency and sober watchfulness,
The grave oppressions that disturb this land.

THE END.

NOTE.

NOTE.

To the brief introduction prefixed to the preceding poem, the notice of a few incidents is added.

The action of the Emperor in the circus at Circejus is taken from Suetonius. The personal exposure and military discipline of Tiberius when in Germany, are related almost in the words of that writer. The cry of "Tiberius to the Tiber," with which the indignant populace received the body of the Emperor, has been anticipated. The fancied address of Apollo, and the sudden fall of the tower of Capri,* are suggested in a passage from the same historian † The arrival of a special deputation from the Senate to salute Caligula, although not historical, is by no means improbable. Its dramatic introduction may be justified as the simplest expression of the universal feeling of hatred and defiance for the dying tyrant, and anxiety for the enthronement of his successor. The rage of Tiberius upon learning the release of certain prisoners by the Senate, and his resolution to hurry to Capri, and there brave his enemies, is taken from the writer already quoted. Both Tacitus and Suetonius name the villa of Lucullus as the place where Tiberius suddenly died. As the latter historian gives several accounts of the manner of his death, and seems equally doubtful about them all, the narrative of Tacitus (as given in the introduction) has been followed. The liberal promises and hearty deter-

* The reader will have noticed that the modern name Capri has been substituted for the *Capreæ* of the ancients.

† Supremo natali suo Apollinem Timenitem et amplitudinis et artis eximiæ advectum Syracusis, ut in bibliotheca novi templi poneretur, viderat per quietem affirmantem sibi, non posse se ab ipso dedicari. Et ante paucos quam obiret dies turris Phari terræ motu Capreis concidit.

minations of reform with which Caligula concludes the drama are strictly in accordance with history. If we can trust Suetonius no prince ever began his reign with a more noble and enlightened policy, or so devotedly attached to his person those whom he governed. A positive insanity has sometimes been suggested as palliating the subsequent atrocities associated with his name.

It can hardly be necessary to remind any reader that the uncertainty regarding a future state of personal existence, attributed to one of the characters at the close of the poem, is supposed to come from one ignorant of Divine Revelation upon that point. Whether a reasonable assurance of such existence is independent of special revelation, is a question upon which the author expresses no opinion—it being sufficient for his purpose that many men of mature judgment and enlarged culture have thought it was not. As answering an objection to the different treatment of this subject in a former drama, it may be worth while to remark, that in an age of simplicity and faith, human beings swayed by the strongest emotion of youth—a passion which in its first intensity seems to bear the impress of immortality—may arrive at conclusions unnatural, in an age of luxury and skepticism, to one long past the period of life when the affections govern and absorb the being.

www.ingramcontent.com/pod-product-compliance
Lightning Source LLC
LaVergne TN
LVHW021430110826
845150LV00007B/2167
9781425507176